The River From My Mouth

The River From My Mouth

poems and paintings by

Karla Van Vliet

Shanti Arts Publishing

Brunswick, Maine

The River From My Mouth

A version of this book was published by
North of Eden Press, 2010
Montpelier, Vermont

Published by Shanti Arts Publishing, 2016
Interior and cover design by Shanti Arts Designs

Cover image: Karla Van Vliet, *The River From My Mouth*

Shanti Arts LLC
193 Hillside Road, Brunswick, Maine 04011
shantiarts.com

Printed in the United States of America

ISBN: 978-1-941830-56-7 (softcover)
ISBN: 978-1-941830-57-4 (digital)

Library of Congress Control Number: 2016950916

To the river.

To the river below and above me,

before and behind me, to the river within me.

To the river that runs from my mouth.

Acknowledgements

The following poems previously appeared in these publications:

Poet Lore: "Iris Open," "First Word," "Thermals," and "What Holds Us Together."

The Deep Well Tapes (North of Eden Press, 2006): "What Makes One," "Revolution," "Yearning," "In Hands,""Seeing Me Through,""Dark Night"under the title "Edge," "The Banished—," "After Departure," "Moment's Sight," "Man At A Distance," "A Though At Twenty Below Zero," "Plank Road," "Blossoms," "Home-coming," "As It Is,"W "The Headwaters," "Love," "Decant," "Flowering," "Exile," "Call To The Beloved," "All I Could Not," and "Becoming The World."

The Secret of the Pomegranate (North of Eden Press, 2007): "Setting Out the Bowl."

Thank you to all who have given me their generous support; you are many and I am grateful for all your kindness. To Christine Cote, special thanks for sponsoring my work in so many ways and by bringing it into the world through Shanti Arts.

Contents

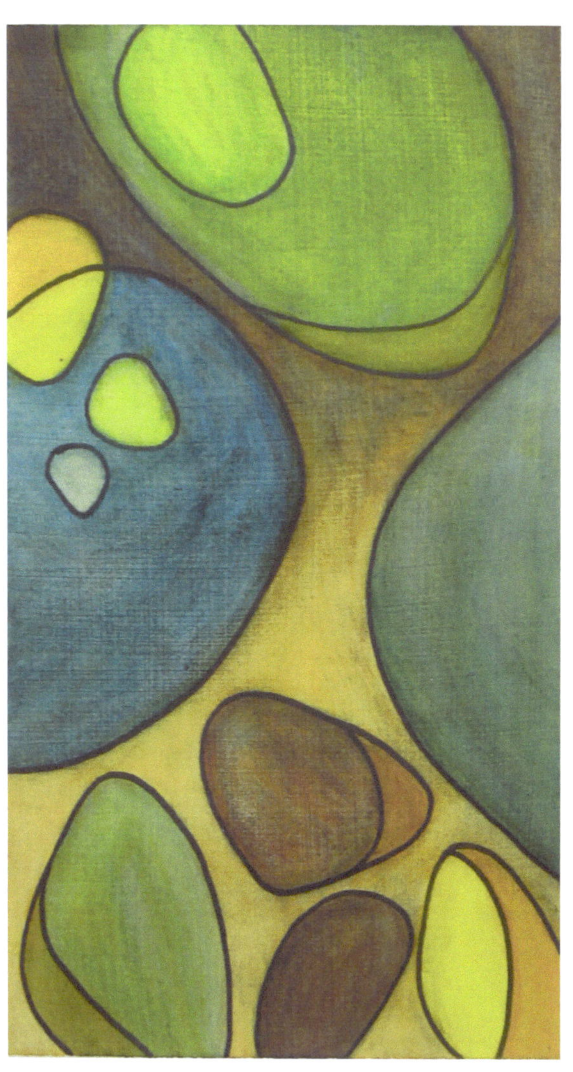

First Word

Every word
runs the hills at night
—W. S. Merwin

This, the first word: raindrop—
touches my face, a laughter,
like the heart's cracking.

This word, the second too.
And from the mountain, the river.
The world has opened its mouth.

This is the beginning.
What comes next, comes by word,
comes by tongue, comes in the bittersweet
of the running river. Against my face.

Thermals

You come home from work,
bone worn, dirty.

Uncountable days now
you've come home.

Still I feel the fluttering
of sparrows.

Still I put down my knitting
at the glide of your foot.

We stand in the shadow
of absent hours,

last night's words pardoned
on both our lips.

Behind you,
blue petals hold their scent.

We draw the wings of our bodies
to one; pause midair.

Iris Open

Irises open their tight blue hearts
in a day, this is how I remember it,
the dark of birth unbolts.

Like thunderclouds or starlings.
Breaking into air.

This is how the heart breaks,
not into pieces, but blue tongues.

A kind of grace
in this disregarding world.

Blue tongues, and at their center,
a yellow star.

Where I Find You

I go out looking for you. The air cold.

Standing outside your house I feel your absence.

You have been a bird, the rain. Once you beat inside me.

Like iron my blood carries your song.

I see a man walking the street's edge.

He is not you.

Between my dream and my hand touching your
sleeve — a quickening.

My celloed body resonates.

I know you most thoroughly by the articulation of
negative space.

When I have held your face in my hand . . . how like a
nestling.

You have been a lake's expanse; my body the boat set adrift.

Where are you.

I unwrap the letters I have written to you, never sent;
fold them to swans.

Now watch, each one lifting onto the wind.

Dark Night

I am led by sound to the river,
by touch to your face.

In the scent of this darkness,
the edge of what is bearable.

Unseeable in the slit night,
the opened flower.

Man at a Distance

You stood beneath the birds,
the clattering of their beaks,
the shadow of their numbers.

What can a moment bring?
I saw you through the house's window
like a painting, Man Listening
to the Thunder of His Soul.

Black strokes over tree's green,
raw canvas road with standing man,
hint of gray sky surfacing below
in puddled foreground.

And what is love if not the seeing clearly
of another's longing?

I went on as if the catch of my breath
was not held in the claw
of whichever bird is your image.

When I turned then turned again,
you had gone.

After Departure

Mist rising from the tree's branches,
like a gown, white and cotton, reveals
the hard nakedness of desire, mine, for you.

And this tree of my body, asks only,
that the wind touch it, as if a hand,
yours, could be imagined.

Umbrage

Since the trees turned
there has been a wind,

a constant, a faithful.

Each tree bending toward
tenderness or fracture.

The heart too, pressing
against din's residency,

will wrench, the sound

like shadow, forcing
the senses taut.

Like the willow
past what it can give.

Seeing Me Through

I turn quickly, to catch
what stands beyond my . . . what's there?

As if, there I stood, bared, bore through
and beckoning my sight to fall on me.

Yes, not quite daring. Daring done by one
sure of being seen, and so . . . what was that?

What is that haunting, halting catch
of wing, shadow of the vacuum?

No, sun reflecting now and in my eye
the tear, I'm sure now, let, no, summoned,

you see, by what I can't . . . nor can I name.

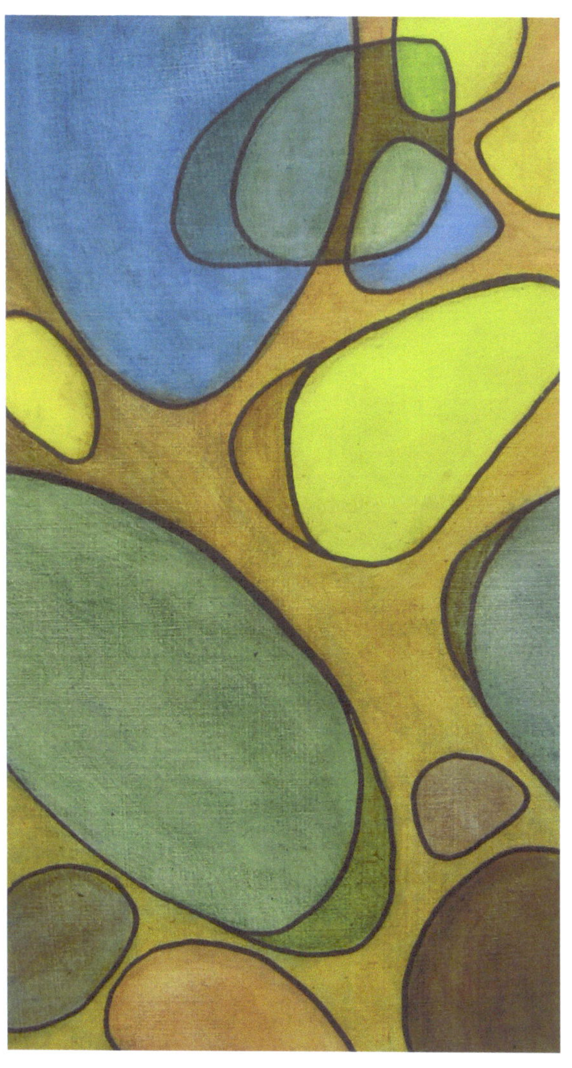

Singing

Air escapes me:
long bone of fingering.

As if song can be held,
my body urging its note.

Enters you, like dust
to cloud, you are falling.

Everywhere, there is you
on my face, like tears.

Song and rain. We cut
a bed in this sweet earth.

Without Sure Knowledge

This is how we have lived for so long—

I know the way doubt fits,
water in a stream bed,
bearing into me.

I am standing under stars,
your window just another light
flickers with curtained forms.

If the warm breeze lasts, I will out stay
darkness, still, at dawn I will enter
my own house to sleep.

If there is reason I have lost it
a marble in the weeds. One day
when you find it, brush away the dirt.

Even now, how can I disregard
the brush of your hand, gesture
of rain against my face?

There is more, but the blue Siberian iris
has blossomed in the dusk of the moon,
the opened mouth of grace.

Blossoms

Some days she drops
the most simple words,

hollyhock blossoms
closed and falling.

She collects them
in a small clay bowl,

twisted and bruised
purple like lips.

The Assembling

Black bodies against the dusky sky.
Above, the crows are assembling.
I stand looking up, nameless against

the storm to come. Their flight
cuts the wind, turns for the tall pines,
one body indistinguishable. Still,

what rumbles beneath the rim of my body,
as if it could escape, as if I would let it,
lifts like a black feathered thing.

The Banished — One Unheard or One Unhearing?

And I, the garden bird,
wing of the underbrush,
spliced song of flower. I am
the shadow's body, the hidden
made flesh, what veers between
the branches of your thoughts.
And look, you are walking away
as if I was not your answer.
Come back, the garden is lonely
for you. The beebalm reddens
as the gaillardia sets sunward.
To your turned back,
I fling my song.

Poem

In the listening, a knife.
A truth that may slay me.

The river, at its edge
like the voice drowning.

Pebble by pebble
it takes down the tree.

You want some story
but there is only this.

No words for the apostate
worth repeating now.

Wolf: The Lure

You have drawn me

fierce along the wooded hill.
My advent feral with hunger,

a bite to your heart.
You know the way—

my night call, the trampled leaves.
So hard forsaking your warm house

to approach what dark conceals.
Fear has its way with us,

you standing in the doorway, me
smelling the gun in your hand.

Wreckage

I didn't want to know you:
empty body, hull, oh you-left-behind.

When I witnessed you at all, was to some
admonishment or jeer I'd set my tongue.

I'd gone, as you recall, for higher ground, dryer.
Or abandoned what adorned in sorrow
I could not stand the smell of: dying fish.
All the same.

To watch you sliver down, sink
into the hungry shallows, you
now gone.

Revolution

Valley: carved by ice
and wave. Sky: forever blue
or gray or starlit. Tell me
this was wanted.

On my tongue: a sliver,
like mint, sharp and disappearing,
your name forgotten.

How silence holds
this body. Clay laid
in the river's curve. Nothing.
Then hands digging in.

This is how we are bared.
What is left: chrysalis hull,
sky torn Common Blue.

Vast soundless valley:
what little whispers I dare make.
To bruise heaven: words thrown
at a sleeping God.

Invocation

Even to utter one small prayer. Bead falling,
red. Or blue, sky at the edge of sight. If ever, one dropped

bead. Inter, but not to ground, see, toward what breaks inside.
Small bead loosened, thread bare. Escape, now salvation.

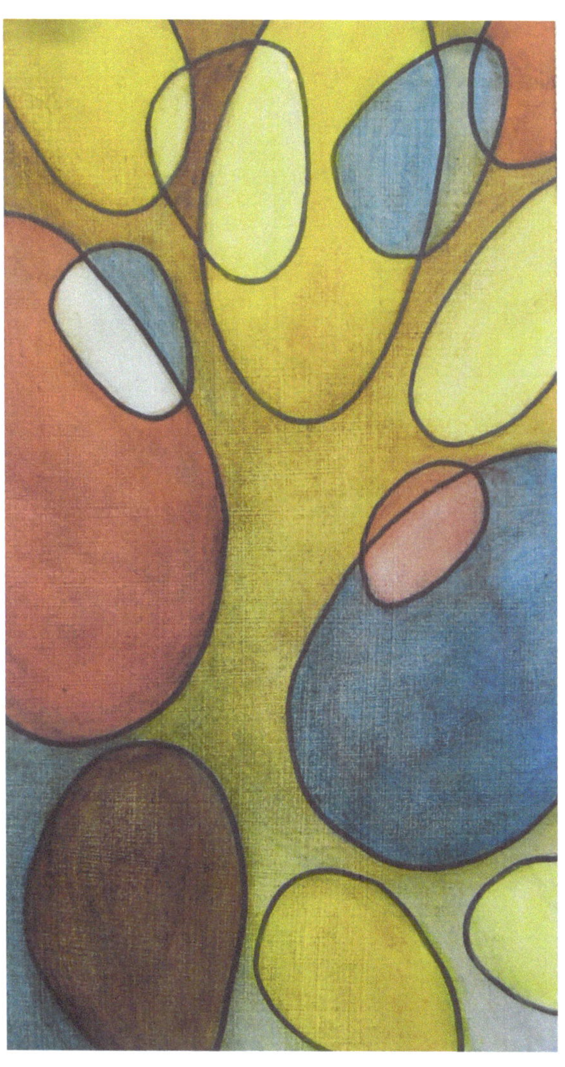

Decant

This rawness beckons
like a wild-thing, wolf,
hawk, newborn babe,
follow the unknown it
says, using the tongue
of water against rock,
its sound like ice to a
burn; so when the night
goes quiet, I think this
silence unbearable,
a burning that might
kill me. Had killed me
once before, a time
I spoke loss fluently.
This time, I open my
mouth, let water pour
the mountain's stream.

What Makes One

Today I opened myself like a jewelry box:
a small ballerina began to dance.

I painted my bathroom green: a cool jungle
in the desert of my home.

Between one mountain range and another:
this great loneliness of separation.

Why do you insist the black lines I scribble
are secrets: as if I would not tell you.

I wonder the distance to the nearest border:
escape involves crossing it, so does salvation.

Chinese plum trees blossom in winter:
red petals like blood against your white white skin.

Once the man I slept beside was struck
by lightning: but it was I who burned him.

Small blue eggs break open:
song emerges from what must live.

Pedro had eyes for a woman with hips,
he could not see me: I did not yet exist.

Far off, beyond the tree lined fields, the yips
of coyotes: yearning melds with night.

If I had words, this is what I would have said:
I am just a little girl, don’t hurt me.

The moon rose over the hill:
some things larger than we understand.

Dreams come each night like rain:
images to be hung on a tree like laundry.

He said, I can no longer be here:
words that should have come from my own lips.

It was simple, without her, I did not know myself:
to love was to be no longer.

The tealeaves read I would break many hearts:
not one more than my own.

Plank Road

Here, at the torn edge. Simple counting,
the slipped threads. Morning held in late snow,
mist rising from the field. Where have I started?

I have memorized the prints of his retreat.
This red thread, woven into my body. Here, and then
there, slipstitched path across the expanse of snow.

I am still counting. Down the road a dog bays,
and now, the near and far answering off the mountain:
the beat of my feral heart.

A Thought At Twenty Below Zero

The door opened, in memory
or to first cold-morning breath, outside
sunrise toward winter east.

Light stained pink sky. And for a moment,
stillness. Recollection. That moment caught. Or say,
frozen, for an instant the gesture held, studied.

What then when the door is closed? New air
within the lungs, turning, the mind changed.
How, in a breath, a life can be altered.

All Blue

A tight blue fist of petals. Opened,
a morning sky's terrible mouth.

What prospect to be contained by:
little bird, speck, soot of the air.

To dance that frantic map
with no point to sight, I am falling.

And again, where can I set my hands,
where, against this body, to catch it?

I had built a scaffolding
but to dismantle a life, what is left to hold.

And now, all blue, all delicate veins, now
skin darkened where I touch.

Crow's Flight

If I lived in the body of the crow
my black wing would cut night's silence.
Black on cold memory. Fall feather of starlit sky.

Oh, wing. Fly toward dawn's suffering.
I will drown in morning song, drown
and awaken bit by eastern light, bit by dew.

If I lived in the body of the crow
my flight would speak the hundred languages of passage,
would suffer my laid out body only to rise and rise again.

Exile

I have not told you, said the girl,
that I lifted above the water's long slip
like a heron

my voice, said the girl, the raw call
of the black bird

when I could not live in you, I lived
in the image of the world

fish in the reeds, black stone
at the river's edge

when you were a border
I was the burnt field, the new grass
lifting through ash

and the fox turning to look,
our eyes meeting.

Red-Bird

Red-bird flits to the maple—
what-cheer, cheer, cheer.
My heart to the tree.

Branches now bare, will no doubt
catch the next spring snow
before budding, spreading green.

Dash of red, then gone.
A thought between fingers.
My turning, my looking away.

Little bird, little red-bird, heart.

All I Could Not

Left words against
this storm's hard edge.

Even now I do not trust
myself to speak.

These words I palm
go warm like stones carried to the river.

See here,
a pyre to set them burning.

In the end, dust or ash,
my throat silted.

Turn from the choked flora
there is no digging out.

Leave it, what's left.
Now, only this new lay of the land.

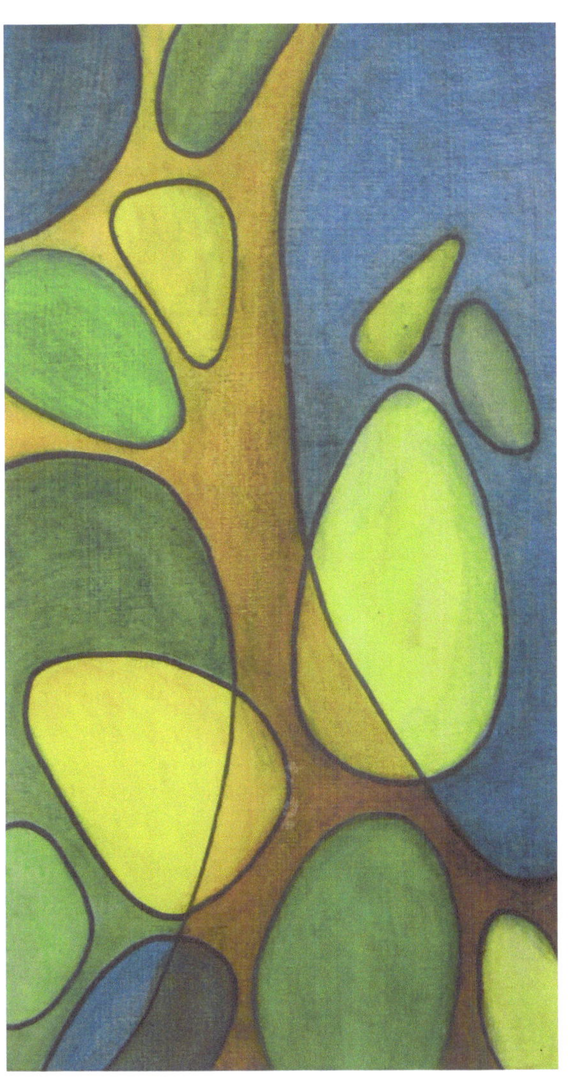

After Rain

Word made of the body,
wet, born, spring let.
The mountain overflowing,

torn down to rock, cataract,
fissure. What scar; inscribed,
the very devotion:

tongue against lip
water coursing a trail
carved out, like change.

See, I am
this wooded hillside, timber
of a song, stream and bed.

Endeavor

The tree's rustle, the crow's, even
the fox's, red with autumn's russet,
what language do I speak now?

My tongue rusty. I fear its hinge.
Truth is like that, buried or laid out
like a ripped dress, the white dress

he ruined. What part do I tell you?
Love, the stained cloth of my body
deceived, my voice branch snagged?

There is nothing but to lay it out.
Sun bleached to white, my bones.
Leave you to read my fortune thrown.

Becoming the World

Then orange light broke over the valley.
Like words, set so long in the territory of the mouth.

Light made sound. Lips seared. I stood.

One must bear the throat's breath, the shiver of leaves
made strange by meaning.

As It Is

There are two ways to live in the world
I have made: walk the fields collecting

dashes of color in my sweaty fist, or dig, dig
the hole I will bury the hunched back of my body in.

Which would you choose, kind sir? The flowers sit
in a vase on the counter, and now in the new darkness,

through the opened window, peepers.

Moment's Sight

After *Ned de Poisson* by Janet Fredericks

The pool's reflection holds
the sky's clouded iris.
In a moment's movement,
near the rushes, I see surface break
of illusion. Fish, thick bodied,
flush the water's darkness
for a moment rise
to the unknowing world.

Fins flutter the reeds of my body.
In its deep pond, fish swim like prayers.

First Bird

I laid the moon in the darkness of my hand,
my body the mystery.

Take what you will.

It is an offering: the water's psalm,
the damp earth bored into.

This is the way to find me,

listen, the first bird has called out
I am here, I am here.

There is nothing new, light
will soon open the east,
love love love there is still time.

In Hands

This is the way it goes:
bird rising through rain,
the sigh of wind-bent grass.

Look here, your touch,
on my reaching hand.

This too, can be love:
rain falling, the earth
catching it like an open palm.

What Holds Us Together

And the dove came in to Noah at eventide;
and lo in her mouth an olive-leaf freshly plucked . . .
—Genesis 8:11

Grasses rise through
the cracked: (words held
under breath, cut out, spilled)
the hard casting of our story.

This is what holds us
together: these fine knives,
green and picked, the slipped
whistle of tongue and air.

This, which demands the fissure,
this, wait, sign. Carried leaf of green.
A birth, or, can I say, I am broke
open like a gate, like the throat in song.

And there is you, (still the waters)
hand put forth for landing.

Homecoming

You come out of the rain,
like a shadow, a bird in flight.

I have missed you,
and this holding you is not enough.

I want to climb into your body's oarless boat
drift into the world looking up into the gray gray sky.

I want the tall pines' hush, the open water
spreading towards the misty horizon.

Call To The Beloved

I bring flowers,

tiger-lilies, like the heart's vase
picked wild.

In the blue sky above, the moon
a dart of brightness.

A bird in the wild apple sings
what with words I say to you —

Come to me, I am here, ready.

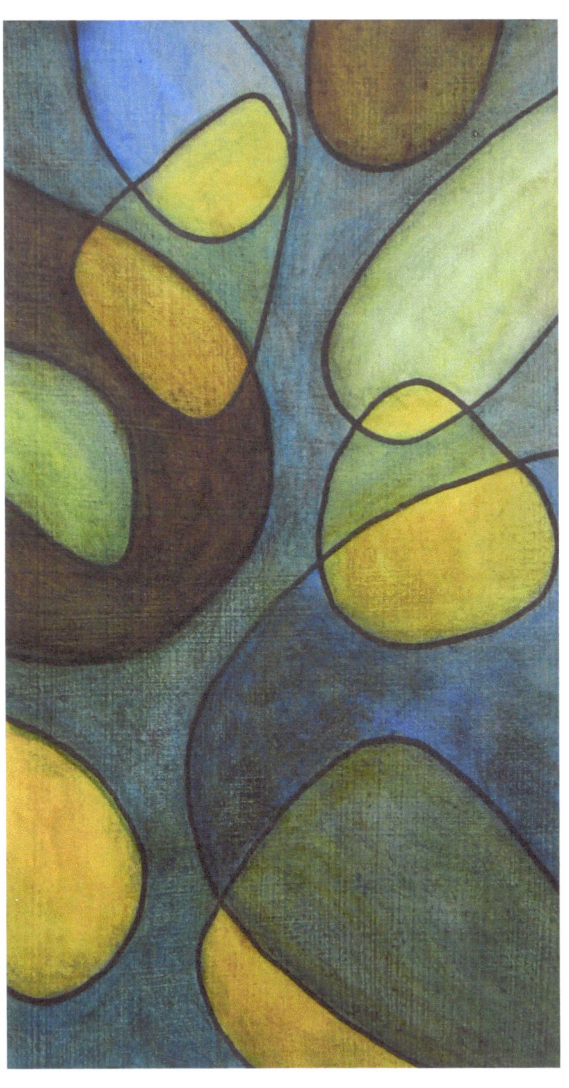

Setting Out the Bowl

I. From the lake-waters
I come, drowned.

I come in faith.

Your hand brushes back the wet hair clung to my cheek,
stills the shudder of my body, turns the weir of my throat
so a thousand waves may break into breath.

I am emptied to the tireless air.

II. The heron lifts free of water.
Gray body pressing

into your dream,
like a hand, reaching—

Like the stream I
cut a place for myself.

When you wake,
remember.

III. It is you I've spelled
    across the pine laid land.
Dark bird, storm along the horizon.

Here is my body
    I have carved for you, a nest.
Body which fits mine, complement.

I want to teach you
    my language blue as sky.
One yet to speak outside the wind.

To live against the night,
    my existence, a terrible hunger,
is to sleep in your twisted arms.

IV. I have this. Folded like a letter,
tied in red string, your words.

Untied, a ribbon of blood to follow
like a trail to your body.

V. I have tired.
Under the sun

lost to branches,
I watch for you.

Lean to the wooded
song of bird, water,

the smallest detail
will alert me.

When the singing dies
my sleep grows restless.

VI. What comes from winter's dreaming
leaves its interpretation like tea in a saucer.

Here, a ladder rises toward dark s`sky,
here, love falls like a leaf toward water.

VII. I come from the sky,
echo blue,

drop upon myself, like rain,
song into an open mouth.

Small bird-bodies lifting
open their shadows across me,

moments of darker blue, rips
into an inner language.

VIII. Here, the mountains reach toward possibility.
At dusk, crows number the uncountable
and move like a thunder cloud.
To the west, light breaks.

IX. Yes, the sky came close,
I am wet to the bone.

What remains against the body,
I love with that dampness.

X. The new green of what lingers underground:
bulb, tuber, intention—

I'll wait.
I have come emptied.

I am the arched abandon
of the bowl set out.

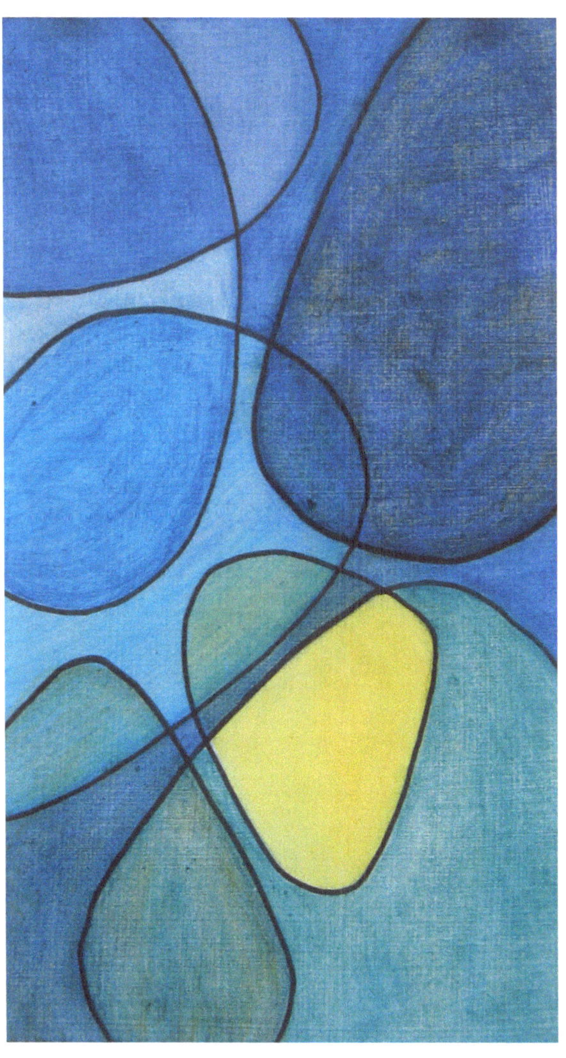

The Headwaters

Spring rising from the deepness
I have dug out. To my lips I bring

what tastes of iron, womb's flood.
I am born here out of near dusk

my breaking over tumbled rock,
the brook from my mouth.

It is enough that I soak the ground
boundaries overflowed, what will grow

from my abundance: forest
with its damp moss, trout lily.

Little yellow star to light my way.

Flowering

I. Earth still holding the bulb
silence from the throat

here song begs to rise

the white stem, trembling
cry from the body split open

this is where it ends, the anticipation
of light, for light

slain darkness the broken ground

I am not crazy to love god.

II. I needn't kill you
if you do not believe

the flower proof enough
pulled open by my fingers

like the slit wound
rent to view heaven

within the body

all is life.

Balancing the Placed Rock

What is known between two people,
dusk-light tethered above the field.

In the valley a heron sights
the crescent of water, follows.

Already, I have dreamt your body
sun-warmed stone. Here, my hand
placed against your chest. Here,

the bird, like heartbeat, sings evening.

Song Beside the Song

Hand stilled,
waxwing above water,
then the hollow
below the shadowed jaw,
breathless brush against blue sky,
skin pressed tight, salt,
grass turned in waxing wind,
marsh-water eyes, fingers
tangled in reedgrass, then sinking,
here, the expansive plane of back,
the tensioned surface drawn
close, tongue to lip's breadth,
to tongue, wings surrendered
against rising thermals, breath held
then lent, the exacting pressure
of submersion, of flight.

After You

Enter the space between breath
and the lung's empty orb: the mouth.
Your finger on my tongue like a whistle bone.

The sound my body makes of yours:
torn dusk, the sky's hollowed bowl.
Night falls, shadowed spell.

Stars escape into the wild notion of
your mouth: an open moon.
In this light, my skin the echo.

Your Hands

If they had been your hands
my body would have been
swallows at dusk

above the pond. Tell me,
how do they move as one
entering night?

Had they been your hands
I would have knelt
like grass in a heavy rain

to the earth. My body
would have come up clean
under the morning sun.

If they had been your hands
my voice would have been
the rush of wind across

the pond. How is it
waves move to the edge of
what holds them?

Had they been your hands
my body would have touched
the prairie with a slim arch

I would have set
the world on fire, the prairie
would have stormed.

What Has Transpired

You are within me now.

My body:

leaf layered ground, deep wood rising to cliffed ridge,
beaver meadow, cedar swamp,
open valley edged by mountain, is lending.

The echo of your footfall has borrowed me.

And I am listening, to hear your beat

by heart:

the timbre of your stride, the pause, division of exhale
from inhale
and your favorite places, the ones returned to, napped in,
the ones left for thought.

Soon, I will have always known you.

Crossing

She steps
into the boat of her ribs.

Nothing now, just the solvent weeping
of water against the hull.

This is night, the way what is left
is only what can be made out.

Now her voice, white petals on the pond,
wind shook apple blossoms.

This, as if reborn the tongue translates
the branch's rustle.

When she steps out of herself
her voice is all of me.

Author and Artist

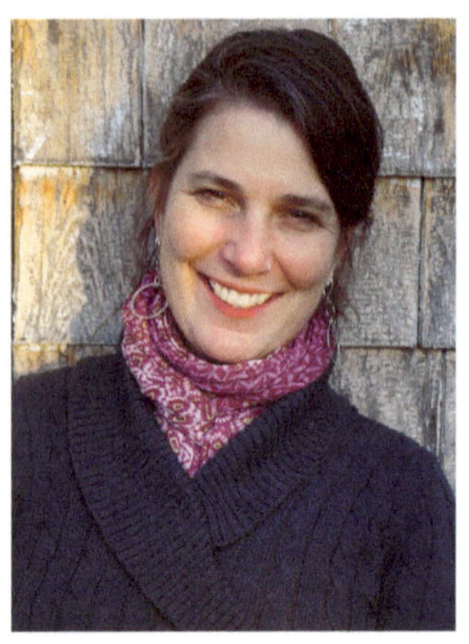
Photograph: Sadie Newman

KARLA VAN VLIET is a poet and artist. *From the Book of Remembrance*, a collection of poems and paintings, was published by Shanti Arts Publishing in 2015. Van Vliet has been nominated for a Pushcart prize, and her poems have appeared in such journals as *Poet Lore*, *Blue Heron Review*, *The Tishman Review*, *Found Poetry Review*, and *Green Mountain Review*. She holds a M.F.A. in poetry from Vermont College of Fine Arts and is co-founder and editor of *deLuge Journal*, a literary and arts journal. She is a Dreamwork analyst and administrator of the New England Young Writers' Conference at Bread Loaf, Middlebury College. Van Vliet lives in Bristol, Vermont.

www.ingramcontent.com/pod-product-compliance
Lightning Source LLC
LaVergne TN
LVHW052307100826
845147LV00006B/695

* 9 7 8 1 9 4 1 8 3 0 5 6 7 *